31 DAYS FOR
ADVENT
FOR SMALL GROUP
OR PERSONAL USE

A Child
is
Born

CWR

Abby Guinness

Acknowledgements

Many thanks are due to my husband, Ben Kinslow. Without his help and encouragement this study guide would not be finished, or even started! It is dedicated to our son, Gabriel, who has taught me so much already. I also want to heartily thank my parents for their invaluable and frequent theological and practical input.

Published 2017 by CWR, Waverley Abbey House, Waverley Lane, Farnham, Surrey GU9 8EP, UK. Registered Charity No. 294387. Registered limited company No. 1990308.

For a list of National Distributors, visit www.cwr.org.uk/distributors

Every effort has been made to ensure that this book contains the correct permissions and references, but if anything has been inadvertently overlooked, the Publisher will be pleased to make the necessary arrangements at the first opportunity. Please contact the Publisher directly.

Concept development, editing, design and production by CWR.

Cover image: istockphoto.com

Printed in the UK by Bishops Printers.

ISBN: 978-1-78259-736-0

Contents

INTRODUCTION

I agreed to write this Advent study guide when I was in the early stages of pregnancy. Now, as I'm writing, I have a baby. Having a child changes everything. I didn't think it would, and neither did my husband, but we knew nothing!

With a baby at close quarters as Christmas approaches, many thoughts about the incarnation have been turning in my mind. Jesus' life made a once-and-for-all, world-changing kind of difference – and He started out just like us. Babies have to learn absolutely everything. I mean *everything*. The fact that God would choose this outrageously vulnerable way to dwell among us is mind-boggling. God put on real flesh, like us.

I can't help but think about those who held Jesus. We hold Him in our hearts and minds, we hold His presence in our lives, but there were people who actually held the baby – *the* baby who was the image of the invisible God (Col. 1:15). How did it affect them?

Considering Bible characters is one of my favourite ways to dig into Scripture and discover its implications for me. (I don't imagine human nature has changed a great deal over the years.) During these 31 sessions I hope you will join me in entering the minds of the people in the Christmas narrative, and a few others. Through them I hope to explore the impact of Jesus coming to earth.

Our four sessions will lead us from the expectation of Jesus' coming, through the physical incarnation, to the repercussions of His presence and the reverberations that rippled out as a result. I think it is important to see the Bible as a whole. It can be too easy to cut it into small pieces and forget how the big picture fits together. Therefore, I have tried to show how the Christmas story is echoed throughout the Scriptures before and after the short Gospel passages that give us the detail of Jesus' early life. Some characters will travel with us throughout the four sessions; others will only appear once or twice. Each day will begin with a little of their story before going on to explore the text a bit more, hopefully providing some food for thought.

Take a moment before you start – ask and expect God to reveal something about Himself to you. Afterwards, you may want to make a note of any thoughts or questions. These could be shared in a group setting for discussion, used as a catalyst for more study, or just kept as a reminder for you to look back on.

Most of all, relax and let your imagination get involved. I hope that, from a grounding in Scripture, our minds can be allowed to wander, which may in turn lead us to wonder. After all, Christmas is a season for wonder! It is a season to marvel at how deeply God understands our humanity and wants to meet us in it. It is a season to look for something new in the stories with which we may feel over-familiar. So humour me, a sleep-deprived, new mum, and may you know the presence, the peace and the wonder of Jesus as vividly as if you were cradling His tiny, swaddled body in your arms.

SESSION ONE

Expectation

DAY 1

Waiting for what is unseen

Opening prayer

Eternal God, help us to hope for what we do not see. Help us to continue building Your kingdom and to wait for its completion with patience. Amen.

Bible reading

Romans 8:22–25

From Abby's perspective

The passage of time in a pregnancy is strange. The first 12 weeks felt agonisingly slow, waiting for the scan that would confirm there was a real life inside. Days of uncertainty stretched unbearably until I knew for sure. Then the weeks felt like they were on fast forward, with hardly enough time to prepare our home (and ourselves) for our baby's arrival. Each day that passed after the due date felt longer than the one before it, and then eventually there was the labour itself, when minutes felt like hours.

I seemed to lose all ability for judging time in those nine months of waiting. Expectation was exciting and it was hard. I felt both elated and terrified. Hope for what was unseen was a very real experience. We were not hoping for something we already had, but for something new. For me, patience came with knowing there would be a lifetime to see the results of the waiting unfold. The expectation was important for our preparation, both practically and emotionally. In many ways, I wish it had been longer, but how much time could ever have been enough?

Waiting is an unavoidable life experience. It can be a difficult experience or a precious one; for some it can even be heartbreaking.

But waiting is very often a part of God's plan. John 1 tells us that Jesus, 'the Word', was present from the very beginning – before 'time' – but thousands of years in the created world passed by before He put on flesh and visited the earth and the people He made.

Throughout the Old Testament, the children of Israel wait for God's redemption plan. We hear much of the expectation and hope for the coming Messiah, as we'll see over the coming days. They didn't know how it would look, and yet they continued to hope for something new.

In today's passage from Romans, Paul chooses to describe us, and the world, as 'groaning in labour pains' while we wait for redemption. Jesus' coming to earth was the beginning of our redemption, and yet we are still waiting for the completion of it.

'Groaning in labour pains' feels an appropriate way to describe expectation for Christmas. When Jesus became human, He didn't take a shortcut – He grew for 40 weeks inside His mother Mary. It is miraculous how new life begins in every case, but even more so in His. Humanity had been waiting for many generations and every year, Advent is a short reminder of the wait God's people endured for His physical coming.

Now, as Paul reminds us, even though we are filled with the Spirit, we are still waiting for the promised return of Jesus. But we are not to expect Him as a baby next time. Revelation tells us He will come 'with the clouds,' and 'every eye will see him' (Rev. 1:7). We live in hope for, and expectation of, that day, remembering that Jesus often told us to be ready and waiting (Matt. 25:1–13).

Ponder

How can you foster a sense of expectation for the coming of Jesus, either remembering His arrival at Christmas, or hoping for His return?

Pray

Pray that hope would be born in those who feel that they have nothing to look forward to this Christmas.

DAY 2

Waiting in darkness

Opening prayer

Eternal God, thank You for sending Jesus, the light of the world. Please enlighten the dark places in our lives. Amen.

Bible reading

Isaiah 9:1–7

From Simeon's perspective

I have been waiting a lifetime. I don't want to die until I have seen the Lord. He has promised I won't, and I trust him. The passage on my lips when I wake every morning is that 'the people walking in darkness have seen a great light'. We need the light.

Mighty God, send us your light!

The darkness here is like shifting shadows, I don't think we know the true difference the full sun would make. We are in the shade of those who rule us, the shade of those we live amongst, in the shade of our fear, the shade of our apathy, the shade of our ignorance. Oh how we will rejoice when he lifts off our oppressors! How I would love to see it; to see the darkness banished in his light.

I'm looking for a child. Will a child with God's authority be obvious? Will I instantly know him? Every firstborn is brought to the temple for thanksgiving. What will happen when the Prince of Peace crosses the threshold? And how long will it be until he can establish his kingdom? How much life will he have to live? What will his justice and righteousness look like? So many questions.

I will keep waiting.

Waiting in the dark.

Waiting for a sunrise.

We'll meet Simeon later in Luke's Gospel, but here we have him considering Isaiah's words. From what we know about Simeon and his love for God and the Scriptures, we can safely assume he was familiar with this passage, written around 700 years before his lifetime. It has been a wait that has stretched over many generations.

Living in a technological age may seem like a blessing or a curse to you, but I love being able to press a switch and be instantly bathed in light. Imagine a long British winter lit by nothing but candlelight... I think I'd go bonkers! Physically dark places can be oppressive. It may be less obvious but surely just as difficult to live in spiritual darkness; even more difficult for those living in the darkness of persecution or enforced enslavement. There are many types of darkness in our world. The Old Testament promises that the coming of Jesus will be the coming of light. In fact, the New Testament echoes and enforces this message. John calls Him the 'True light that gives light to everyone' (John 1:9).

Today's passage from Isaiah ascribes to Jesus multiple majestic names, each one a marker of His being God. The grandeur contrasts with the simplicity of a human child being born, a son being given. The word 'given' reminds us of what we often consider at Christmas – that His presence is a gift to us. The light that He brings is a gift to those struggling in the dark – a waiting expectation full of hope.

Ponder
In what ways has knowing Jesus brought light to your life? Are there ways you can show that light to others?

Pray
Pray for those you know who feel like they are in the dark, or who are waiting for answers.

DAY 3

Waiting for justice

Opening prayer

Eternal God, help us to trust that You will bring justice. Make us teachable, so that we may treat others justly. Amen.

Bible reading

Isaiah 42:1–9

From Anna's perspective

I hope I have been God's servant. I have served him as faithfully as I am able. I like to think of serving him as waiting on him. I try to hear and understand what would please him, which can take some time, then I attempt to fulfill those wishes. But I am not the servant. No one is waiting to hear from me. Imagine what we could learn if we could hear God speak to us directly! If he were to stand in this temple court and teach us what he knows! Would we listen? Would we understand? I don't know if justice can be understood, but I am glad that he will bring it. There seems to be so little of it around. Waiting for justice must be the toughest kind of waiting. Will he show us how to act justly? How many people would have to catch his message to make a difference? If he will not lift up his voice in the street then how will his message spread? We must trust that he will not stop until it happens. And, I guess, continue to wait on him when he has come and after he has gone.

We find Anna in Luke's Gospel, with Simeon. I have given her more of Isaiah's words to ponder, from later in his writing. Although these verses describe Jesus quite differently to yesterday's passage from chapter 9, similar language appears. Jesus is 'given' to the people as a 'light' to the nations (Isa. 9:6). We also hear mention of the

Lord doing a 'new' thing, which Paul encouraged us to hope for in our reading on Day 1. I would suggest that the echoes in Scripture are caused by how familiar the many writers were with its varied content, and of course by God's sovereign inspiration of it. It ends up being like a puzzle with many pieces fitting together to create one beautiful image of God's eternal masterpiece.

Justice is a recurring theme that we will hear more about. It resounds through this passage, and fulfills the names given to Jesus earlier; the Prince of Peace, with what is variously translated 'government' or 'authority' on Him, and could be understood as sovereign leadership. The Hebrew root word is about power and the right to rule. It is reassuring to hear that someone with that power would be just, righteous and full of God's glory, as this passage promises.

I love the mention in verse 4 of the coastlands waiting for His teaching. It reminds me to cherish the teaching of Jesus to which we have access through the Gospels. In our contemporary culture we may find decision-making tricky on matters of self-conduct in our contemporary culture, but having the words of Jesus should certainly help.

Ponder

Do you find the teaching of Jesus affects how you treat others?

Pray

Pray for those suffering injustice, and for those in our country and around the world who aim to protect people by establishing and upholding our legal systems.

DAY 4

Waiting for one who is already here

Opening prayer

Eternal God, thank You that You are present in our past and our future. Remind us that You are with us now. Amen.

Bible reading

Micah 5:2–4 (NRSV)

From a chief priest's perspective

Bethlehem, of all places! But then the God of Israel does seem to root for the underdog, so perhaps it's the obvious choice. I've discovered that whatever is least expected shall the Almighty favour. That sounds like a scripture! Bethlehem: House of Bread. And the one born there shall 'feed his flock'. Makes sense actually. Like manna in the wilderness.

Studying the holy writings is a surprisingly fun part of being a priest. We read, think, sit and discuss. We argue a great deal of the time. My wife calls it 'hot air'. But these words are not air. They speak of life and flesh and solid things that have been, and are, and will be. Micah's words pull together the past, present and future by talking of the one who will come to rule, but yet comes from ancient days. Then it says 'now' he 'shall be' great. That's one to argue about. Grammar is always a favourite disagreement. What's that 'now' doing in there? When shall he be great? In ancient days, and in the future when he rules, and now? But where is he now? We are waiting for a baby to be born who is apparently already ruling. A complex thing, these Scriptures. Now you see why it is a full-time job to study them. Perhaps I should keep an ear to the ground in Bethlehem. Actually, that's crazy talk – we've been waiting so long I doubt it'll happen any time soon.

And I'm sure I'll hear when it does. Probably won't even be in my lifetime,
which means we may as well continue our arguments without him.

Micah was a contemporary of Isaiah, also writing around 700 years
before Christ. In Matthew's Gospel, when Herod gathers the scribes
and chief priests to discover where the new ruler is to be born, it is
from this Scripture that they know it will be Bethlehem, described
as 'little', and meaning 'house' or 'place' of bread. Bethlehem is
mentioned earlier in the Bible as the home of those in the ancestry
of Jesus – Naomi, Ruth and Boaz, Jesse and David. The mention of
His origin being 'from ancient days' could refer to the long heritage
of His people. We hear that Jacob was on the way to Bethlehem
when his wife Rachel died (Gen. 48:7). This majestic ruler of Israel
shall be a member of their own family.

In addition, the 'old origin' of Jesus is of course that He existed even
before the earth. The sentence 'now He shall be great' in verse 4 is
directly translated from the Hebrew. I like the way it plays with our
concept of time. It reminds me that God need not be bound by time as
we understand it. Jesus is able, as God, to be the one 'who is, and who
was, and who is to come' (Rev. 1:8).

Ponder

Do you enjoy studying and discussing the Scriptures, or do you find
it difficult? What might help?

Pray

Pray for the leaders of the churches in your area – that they would
continue to be able to make studying the Bible a priority.

DAY 5

Waiting with perseverance

Opening prayer

Eternal God, thank You that You hear our prayers. May we listen for Your response, whatever it might be and whenever it might come, with open hearts. Amen.

Bible reading

Luke 1:5–17

From Zechariah's perspective

Being a priest is an honour. I do my best to honour God, both in the temple and in my daily life. My section has been on duty many times but this was the first time the lot fell on me. My turn to offer incense, after all these years. I felt a little overawed. The sound of the prayer washing in from those outside the sanctuary was comforting.

Then, as if the moment was holy and terrifying enough, the dazzling face of the Lord's angel was before me. I could hardly make out his features for the blaze of light shining out from him. I wanted to run but I feared my ancient legs wouldn't carry me far or fast enough. He said that our prayer had been heard. Our seemingly endless and ongoing prayer for a child had reached the ear of God and our waiting wouldn't be in vain. Elizabeth will have a son and we will know joy, gladness and rejoicing. We will be parents to a son who will be filled with the Spirit and will turn the people of Israel to the Lord!

It is beyond what we asked for, it is our secret thoughts heard as well as our public hurt healed – but not in any way I could have foreseen. My visit to the sanctuary was not what I expected. How could I have imagined this outcome to all the years that came before? I can't picture Elizabeth's face when I tell her. Our son will make this people ready for the Lord. That means the Lord is coming, and soon –

it is proof of countless, endless prayers that have come to the ear of our God. He is coming.

The priests serving in the temple served in teams or 'divisions' set up by Hezekiah (and detailed in Chronicles). All would have various duties such as burnt offerings, peace offerings, praise and prayer (2 Chron. 31:2). In addition they would draw lots to select which individual would go into the 'Holy of Holies', the innermost sanctuary of the temple, to burn incense to the Lord. I like the way God orchestrates some 'alone-time' with Zechariah in this sacred space.

The arrival of John the Baptist, a son to Zechariah and Elizabeth, is an answer to both personal and communal prayers. God hears the couple who long to be parents, just as He hears the nation longing for a Saviour. We are told that Zechariah and Elizabeth are righteous and live blamelessly before God (v6). Not so the people of Israel at large who need their hearts turning from disobedience in order to be prepared for the arrival of the Lord (v17). Whatever state we are in, however we are living, God still hears and comes to meet us.

Ponder

Are there any prayers that you have been praying for a long time? Or prayers that you have given up praying? Do you think God is still listening?

Pray

Pray for those who are longing for breakthrough. Intercede for those who might have given up praying for things such as healing, reconciliation, or perhaps a family of their own.

DAY 6

Waiting for the miraculous

Opening prayer

Eternal God, may we be open to all You can do and willing to be surprised. Help us to look forward with hope and expectation. Amen.

Bible reading

Luke 1:18–25

From Gabriel's perspective

It's an exciting time for me. Three announcments at once! It's hard for a messenger to keep his lips buttoned when he's desperate to shout his exciting proclamation. 500 years ago I chatted with Daniel and dropped a hint. 500 years! And now finally I'm allowed to tell it like it is. The anointed one is ready and earthbound. Zechariah first, Mary next… Joseph might need a quick visit too.

I was a bit surprised Zechariah wasn't instantly convinced. I'm Gabriel! I told him, 'I stand in the presence of God!' (I would have thought that was obvious by the shiny face.) So I struck him dumb for a little while. It's only temporary. I just thought he needed to keep his mouth a bit more shut and his mind a bit more open to what the Lord can do. To what the Lord will do, especially now that the anointed one is on the way. Perhaps Elizabeth will thank me. Don't worry, he'll be talking again when John arrives – he won't be able to keep from shouting about what's to come. By which time I'll be sitting with a front-row seat to watch with excitement as the sovereign plan continues to unfold!

In the book of Daniel (chapters 8 and 9) there are prophetic visions that are tricky for Daniel to understand. Gabriel is sent to help him decipher the apocalyptic imagery. It requires much deeper study from modern readers to work out all the references, time bands and what is being described. However, in Daniel 9:25–26, there is mention of 'the Anointed One' who will be 'put to death and have nothing' – which is certainly a reference to the coming of Jesus. 500 years later, Gabriel visits Zechariah to announce the arrival of John the Baptist, before going to Mary to tell her about the conception of Jesus.

I like his simple statement – 'I stand in the presence of God'. In Exodus 34 we hear that the skin of Moses' face shines because he has been talking with God, so imagine the shining face of one who dwells constantly in His presence. Added to which, people always seem afraid when an angel appears; perhaps it is their exceptional luminescence.

We hear that Zechariah is struck dumb because he did not believe Gabriel's words (v20). I find it completely normal that he would ask how something so unexpected and out of the ordinary might be possible. We all find it hard to believe that the boundaries of nature can be so stretched when God chooses to act. But then that is how we know He is at work.

Ponder

Do you expect God to work beyond what should be possible by earthly standards? How could we be open to seeing Him work outside of our expectations?

Pray

Pray for those who feel that they need a miracle beyond standard expectation – perhaps one of healing or provision.

DAY 7

Waiting for the unexpected

Opening prayer

Eternal God, may we learn to accept Your will and serve You accordingly in every circumstance. Amen.

Bible reading

Luke 1:26–38

From Mary's perspective

I have a secret. It wants to explode out of me but I'm too scared. I met an angel! But that's not the secret. Something's going to happen, he told me. It might have happened already… I don't even know, I can't feel it! But I won't be able to hide it for long…

Who will believe me? A 'holy child' is the last thing they'll call him!

Why would my God come to me? I said I was at his service. I've always said I would do whatever would please him. I never thought for a moment… I mean, who would think he would ask for this? How could I imagine? God's son, carried to earth like this! Forty weeks, or thereabouts. I will have to wait to see – to see if what the messenger said was true. How many symptoms will make me believe it? How large will I have to grow? Nothing will be impossible with God, he said. Well this would certainly prove it.

Is the time finally here? After all these generations? I thought it was still a distant hope. Will this be the one we've been waiting for? And what if he actually is the one? How will I protect him? How can I teach him anything at all? How will I know what to do?

Deep breaths, Mary. One day at a time. Just one day. Nothing will be impossible with God, the angel said. Except maybe waiting patiently to see what happens. And then raising a child who is God. How will I do that? And why on earth did I tell him I would?!

Mary says, 'I am the Lord's servant… May your word to me be fulfilled' (v38). She is willing to do whatever God asks of her, and this is a pretty 'out there' request! If you stop to think about it, what she offers to the Lord here is immense. There is the risk of losing her intended marriage to Joseph (or any other prospective husband), the risk of losing family and friends, the laying down of her reputation, her body, the years needed to raise a child, her whole lifetime. This is no half measure of commitment. Of course there is blessing in it, as well as pain, and we'll come to the impact of that in due course. But at this stage, I wonder at her willingness to give everything up for the unknown, trusting in God's purposes.

Gabriel has told her that her cousin Elizabeth is also expecting – another miracle! – and we hear in the following verses that she takes the opportunity to go and visit immediately. Perhaps she needs to go somewhere, to do something, to connect with someone about what has happened. It seems a wise choice to go to someone who is 'in' on the godly nature of these happenings and is on the same page. Serving God is easier done with others than alone.

Ponder

Do you think there are limits to what you'd be willing to do in the Lord's service? Would you do anything? What do you think He is asking of you today?

Pray

Pray for those serving the Lord in difficult circumstances – perhaps missionaries at home or abroad – particularly those who are struggling to keep going.

DAY 8

Waiting for forgiveness

Opening prayer

Eternal God, thank You for Your forgiveness. Help us to become more like You every day. Amen.

Bible reading

Matthew 1:18–25

From Joseph's perpsective

This isn't quite how I pictured the start of our marriage. An angelic visitation. A message from the Lord. A conception by the Holy Spirit. A child we will raise on behalf of the Almighty before we've had a chance to practice on any of our own. It felt easier when my quiet escape was planned. Now I'm in for the long haul.

I don't think I would have believed the dream was anything more than bad cheese, except the angel told me the baby's name. It was the same one Mary had already said, Jesus. The Lord saves. He will save us from our sins.

A sinless child will be a challenge, for sure. Exposing. I'm bound to have more sins ahead of me than behind, however hard I try. And I've been told that being a parent makes everyday patience and kindness so much harder to achieve, despite the extra practice.

What kind of role model will I be? Perhaps, just maybe, a little of him will rub off on us. That would be good. Perhaps being around him will help me hit the mark more often. That's something to hope for, at least.

In this passage we are told that the naming of Jesus is important. We get the anglicised form of His name from the Greek, *Iesous*. In Hebrew it is *Yeshua* or *Yehoshua*. It comes from the root word meaning 'deliver' or 'rescue'. The fact that He will rescue humanity from sin, is Jesus' identity and what God wants to be clearly known.

In Greek the passage literally reads, 'for He shall be saving His people from their misses'. 'Misses' seems a good way to think of our sin. It is all the ways we have failed to hit the target of right-living. Romans 3:23 tells us that 'all have sinned and fall short of the glory of God.' In comparison, Jesus will remain the only human to be sinless. Hebrews 4:15 says of Him, 'For we do not have a high priest who is unable to feel sympathy for our weaknesses, but we have one who has been tempted in every way, just as we are – yet he did not sin.'

The Jewish people made sacrificial offerings as detailed in the Torah (the first five books of the Old Testament). These provided atonement for sin. After Jesus had died and risen, these were no longer necessary as He was the ultimate sacrifice to provide forgiveness. For those of us living in the light of this salvation, forgiveness can seem straightforward because we have accepted the grace of God, which is so freely given (it doesn't seem to make it any easier to avoid future sin, but we should try). In this season of waiting, let's remember those still waiting for their salvation, who may feel burdened by the baggage of their 'misses'.

Ponder

How can we be intentional about being less sinful tomorrow than we are today?

Pray

Pray for those battling addictions or hard-to-break habits, that unwanted chains would be broken.

SESSION TWO

Incarnation

DAY 9

God our Father

Opening prayer

Present God, we praise You, our Father, for Your willingness to meet us in our frail humanity. Amen.

Bible reading

John 1:14–18

From John the disciple's perspective

That my eyes have seen God's glory still gives me shivers. The face I know so well, the face of my friend, is the face of the Son of God. Jesus, the anointed one, has made God known. In so many ways he has taught us what God is like. He used words, told stories, asked questions. He acted, set an example. He was the very embodiment of truth and grace. God in human form.

It blows my mind to think that he was there before this world began. He wouldn't boast, but I think I caught a cheeky glint in his eye from time to time. 'There's nothing new under the sun,' he would joke when we were all mind-boggled at something he'd said or done that felt like nothing we'd ever seen or heard before.

I had never really thought of God as the Father before. Father of the nation, of course, but my father? Not until Jesus started to talk about him like that, like he was right there with us the whole time. When he left, he said he was going 'to my father and your father.' We share the same Father. That makes him my kind-of brother. I like that. Who better to help me know the Father better? To know more of his grace and truth. It floors me every time I think about it.

Incarnation is the key theology of Christmas and the source of my thoughts throughout this study. The awe-inspiring mystery of God choosing to become fully human fascinates me. As *The Message* translates it, 'The word became flesh and blood and moved into the neighbourhood' (John 1:14) This Bible passage is probably the best known and most quoted on the topic.

Within today's four verses, right at the start of his Gospel, John mentions God as the Father twice. In fact, he goes on to refer to God as Father over 100 times during the course of his Gospel. God is mentioned as Father in the Old Testament very little – occasionally as the Father of the nation of Israel, and sometimes of some of the patriarchs, but it is Jesus that begins the regular use of that name for God and encourages His followers to address God as such. John stresses that Jesus is the 'only' son, even though God is Father to us all. The Bible is full of such nuances for us to grapple with!

The other word that is repeated in these lines is 'grace'. It appears three times in the NIV translation, and four times in others. It is through Jesus that God's grace becomes accessible to us, and so John stresses this 'grace upon grace' (John 1:16, NRSV) that we receive through Him. This grace is again more regularly talked about in the New Testament than the Old, now that Jesus has come to make it known. It is love and mercy, undeserved and unearned that is given freely nonetheless.

Ponder
Do you think of God as Father and Jesus as brother? Which do you relate to more often? Are they helpful descriptions for you?

Pray
Pray for those who want to know God, that they would be drawn to Him through Jesus.

DAY 10

Sacrificial God

Opening prayer

Present God, inspired by Your example, may we put the needs of others before our own. Amen.

Bible reading

Philippians 2:3–11

From the apostle Paul's perspective

Regarding others as better than yourself is tricky. Maybe we're wired for self-protection but letting go of my own interests is probably one of the hardest things I've tried. I don't think I'll ever manage to let go of them completely but my aim is to at least consider the interests of others to be more important than mine.

I'm an ambitious man. I strive to be better and work as hard as I can to be more like Christ. But I don't want to get there alone. I want others to come with me. Otherwise, what are my ambitions worth? But thinking I can lead or drag others with me is foolish. Many are further ahead than I am, and all can teach me something. My ambition must be to listen and to serve, with Christ as my example.

When you hear the stories of his birth (Mary tells a great tale), you realise how willing he was to 'slum it', to welcome anyone and everyone, to take life as it comes, to prioritise God's purposes over any stuff he might want. Always putting the needs of other people before himself, inviting them in, from the beginning to the end. Lord, make me more like that!

Paul explores the leap that Jesus had to make in coming to earth – equal with God and yet becoming a servant. He was subject to the same weaknesses as we are and had to face the same risks.

Yesterday we read John's description of the glory of Jesus, and here Paul describes how Jesus 'emptied' Himself of that glory in His willingness to be like us.

The Christmas story is full of humility and grim reality – born amongst animals, laid in a feeding trough, visits from shepherds, life on the run and years as an asylum seeker in Egypt. We don't have the heavenly starting point that Jesus did – so there is far less to sacrifice! Yet preferring the needs of others is probably one of our greatest human challenges.

Advent is a good time to consider how to look to the interests of others. While buying gifts for family members, are there others in need that you could bless at the same time? Could you consider ethical or Fairtrade presents? Is there a night shelter in your town for those sleeping rough at this cold time of year? Could you reduce your Christmas budget in order to give more away? Could you entertain strangers and neighbours as well as friends? Could you visit the elderly or seek out the lonely and invite them to join you? All of these things, taking thought, effort and some measure of sacrifice, will pour blessing on others, and probably bless you as well.

Ponder
On a daily basis, and in practical terms, what might it look like to put the needs of others before your own?

Pray
Pray for those living in humble circumstances, that the kindness of others would bless them this Christmas.

DAY 11

God's family tree

Opening prayer

Present God, human and divine, divinely inspire our human reading of Your Word. Amen.

Bible reading

Luke 3:23–38 or Matthew 1:1–17

The genealogy of Jesus is included by Matthew and Luke in both their Gospels. However, their lists differ quite substantially about five generations past Abraham and again after David. This has been the source of much debate over many years. Some say that one is Mary's line as the blood relative and the other is Joseph's, as the legal father. Some suggest the differences are due to the practice of siblings marrying widows, making biological and legal patronage quite different. It has been used by some to try and discredit the Gospels completely.

I started to write a piece making conjecture about the writing process for Luke or Matthew. I have read that Jewish record-keeping was meticulous, but I don't know how the writers discovered or compiled the list and where they would have sourced their information. I didn't feel my guesses would be anywhere close to plausible. So I have declined to comment in that way today!

I feel that, much like the creation story in Genesis 1, this genealogy is not meant to be a scientifically accurate exercise. There is an important reason for including the human lineage of Jesus, whether you know the precise details or not. Matthew and Luke are making the same point: Jesus is not only God, He is also decidedly human. He did not just appear from nowhere, He was not an alien or a ghost, He was descended from human flesh and had ancestors. Luke takes the line all the way to Adam, the first human. Including the bloodline also demonstrates, importantly, that this is part of God's big story, not an isolated moment in history.

The other vital point they are making, and both writers agree here, is that this is King David's family tree. Both agree on David's immediate heritage of Boaz, Obed and Jesse. Matthew suggests that it carries on with David's son Solomon; Luke suggests that it's through Nathan. But it doesn't really matter which of David's sons it was, because in order for readers to understand that Jesus is the anointed one – the promised one – the important thing is that He is descended from David. There are so many prophecies throughout the Old Testament promising that the Messiah would come from David's descendants. Psalm 89 in particular talks of God's promise to David: 'I will establish your line forever' (vv4,29,36).

These points concerning Jesus' lineage are also key to Paul's theology. He opens Romans with the description of Jesus as God's Son who 'as to his earthly life was a descendant of David' (Rom. 1:3). Later, in Romans 5, he pulls together the big picture of how sin entered the world through one man, Adam and salvation came through one man, Christ. This is reiterated in 1 Corinthians 15:22: 'as in Adam all die, so in Christ all will be made alive.'

The Bible, and faith in Jesus, can be mind-boggling. But the fact that Jesus is both fully divine and fully human – the incarnation – is at the heart of our overwhelming God.

Ponder

Do you think the Bible is to be taken literally? Where have your best moments of understanding come from?

Pray

Pray that all would be inspired by the Spirit while reading the Bible and find help to understand it deeper.

DAY 12

God with us

Opening prayer

Present God, fill me with Your Spirit today, that I might have confidence to share what I know about You. Amen.

Bible reading

Isaiah 63:7–9; Luke 1:39–45

From Elizabeth's perspective

Feeling a baby move inside you is the strangest thing. What a blessing that God would grant me this when I had thought all hope was lost! The rolls and punches are reassuring. Sort of comforting. Except when I'm trying to sleep and he seems to be rehearsing a gymnastic routine! It makes it feel so real when part of a little body presses against the surface. Slightly alien, maybe, especially under my wrinkles, but really real. What I felt today was different – it was like he turned a full cartwheel and I was overwhelmed with a rush of peace and joy and the words tumbled out of me that Mary and her baby are blessed. So blessed!

God is surely on the move… the barren womb conceives, the virgin is with child, the time has come! It's happening, it's real!

'Hope deferred makes the heart grow sick', is what King Solomon wrote, and I have felt sick in so many ways. Would I say that I lost hope over all those years? Hope that I would be a mother? Yes. Hope that God can do anything? No. I have always known that he will fulfill his promises. Finding my part to play in it has been my delight.

The new covenant begins… Mary's child is the anointed one and our child shall make it known. I don't feel scared anymore. Prophet Isaiah's words are ringing in my ears – I remember God's mercy, his love and his favour and that it is by his presence that he saves us.

He is here! He has come!

I have chosen to have Elizabeth remember Isaiah 63:7–9, particularly as translated by the NRSV (italics added for emphasis):

'I will recount the gracious deeds of the LORD, the praiseworthy acts of the Lord, because of all that the Lord has done for us, and the great favour to the house of Israel that he has shown them according to his mercy, according to the abundance of his steadfast love… and *he became their savior in all their distress. It was no messenger or angel but his presence that saved them*; in his love and in his pity he redeemed them; he lifted them up and carried them all the days of old.'

Elizabeth understands that God's promises are being fulfilled and her story is full of the same words: mercy and favour. Also, the key factor here about God being our Saviour is His presence. The incarnation grants His physical presence, as well as the spiritual kind.

Shortly after these verses, Isaiah 63:11 speaks of the Holy Spirit being put within the people, and this is what Elizabeth experiences. Zechariah was told that John would be filled with the Spirit before he was born (Luke 1:15), and here we see it happen as soon as the only-just-conceived Jesus comes near (Luke 1:39–45). If Elizabeth has been in hiding until now, I wonder if it is the presence of the Spirit with her that gives her the confidence to face the public scrutiny of an unusual pregnancy and begin to talk of what God has done.

Ponder

Do you think being filled with the Spirit is necessary to sense the presence of God?

Pray

Pray for those who would like to know the presence of God, that they would experience His love.

DAY 13

Joyful God

Opening prayer

Present God, I choose to rejoice at Your coming. Please give me Your joy in my soul. Amen.

Bible reading

Luke 1:46–56

From Mary's perspective

It's real now. I know it's happening. Elizabeth's greeting took me by surprise – she knew! She knew the baby was there and who he was. And her baby knew too, apparently. It has finally sunk in – this is really happening. God's child is growing in my womb and it is an honour and a blessing and I don't know why he chose me but he did. I've got this deep joy bubbling up out of me, which makes a nice change from the nausea.

I have always enjoyed the Jewish practice of recounting what God has done for us. I love to remember the exploits of our ancestors and the way he intervened. I love the deserts and the seas, the fires and clouds, the armies and angels, generations and dynasties, the goodies and baddies, mistakes and triumphs, and God's unending, inexhaustible mercy. And I can't quite get my head around this but, as that continues, years from now, I'll be part of it. I'm in the story. What did I do to deserve it? Nothing! But I will be known as blessed for all the generations to come because of the child I'm carrying. I'd better not mess it up. Good job God won't leave me now. Vested interest.

Elizabeth's response to Mary's arrival may have been the first confirmation Mary had, and certainly a great second opinion on what Gabriel had told her. The two women, one young and one old, are sharing in the plans of God in an extraordinary way. Much like Paul's comments on humility, both women state their lowliness. They major on the mercy of God in choosing their involvement.

Miracle pregnancies have been seen in the story of Israel before. In the Old Testament, Hannah (mother of Samuel) along with Sarah (mother of Isaac) had late and miraculous conceptions. Each time God intervenes in this way, the child goes on to play an important part in the history of God's people. They know that something special is happening, not least because Gabriel has been sent to give them the heads-up.

Mary echoes thoughts from Hannah's prayer in 1 Samuel 2:1–10. Either God inspires the same spontaneous praise or, more likely, Mary was familiar with the Scriptures. Perhaps portions were set to music and sung, or perhaps she had spent lots of time listening to them read aloud. Mary improvises around the words of the Old Testament, not just from 1 Samuel but themes from the Law and the Psalms as well. It is so full of emotion and enthusiasm that the words alone paint a clear picture of her deep joy. She says that her 'soul' magnifies God. If it is joy in her soul, then it must be that rejoicing in His goodness is enough to magnify God and bring praise to Him. The coming of Jesus is certainly something to rejoice about – and Christmas a wonderful time to spread that joy!

Ponder

Can you rejoice even if you don't feel like it? Considering Mary's words, how do you think joyfulness could be inspired?

Pray

Pray for those who may feel that joy is beyond them at the moment, that they would be able to rejoice in the Lord.

DAY 14

God in the flesh

Opening prayer

Present God, help us to look beyond our surroundings and to avoid materialism. Amen.

Bible reading

Luke 2:1–7

From Joseph's perspective

I don't imagine it was the birthing experience most women would want. Thank you Emperor Augustus for the census. Wonderful timing.

Early or late, that baby was arriving in Bethlehem and we had to make the best of it. We hadn't been able to carry much, so relied on the kindness of others and improvisation.

I've never been so grateful for the way women rally around and spring into action – I was happy to be bossed around by a hundred fussing relatives I haven't met before. I fetched buckets of water, clean straw, more cloths. When the instructions stopped I took it upon myself to use some spare cloth to fashion some curtains across our little corner. At least a little privacy. Torchlight certainly helped improve the ambience although it didn't disguise the smells. We'll call it 'rustic'. A makeshift crib in humble surroundings. He seemed cosy and Mary didn't seem to mind. I guess her concentration was elsewhere.

When the gaggle finally gave us some peace (about two days later) it was the best bit. Just the three of us, Mary and me staring at this tiny baby boy who had no idea where he was. Maybe that's a good thing…

There is no mention of a stable anywhere in the Bible. The only specific we have is the manger (an animal feeding trough) where Jesus was laid. We are also told this was the case because there was no place in the inn. The word translated as 'inn' is *katalumati* and is also translated as 'guest room'. The word only appears in one other place in the New Testament – it refers to the room where Jesus would eat the Last Supper with His disciples. (It is interesting that His first and last days on earth are paralleled.) The guest room would have been within the living quarters of a private house. Luke 22:11–12 describes it as an upstairs room and tells us it is large and furnished. However, downstairs, people kept their animals indoors to keep them safe and warm at night. Therefore it's likely that they were still accommodated with family, but not in the upstairs living quarters. (When the magi visit they are in a 'house' – Matt. 2:11.) Downstairs would have been farming equipment, perhaps cooking facilities, animals and so on – a kind of working utility area. I've heard many guesses about whether family members refused to put them up due to the pre-marital pregnancy, or whether the town was just too full to accommodate everyone, or perhaps older members of the family got priority. There are plenty of theories and we have no way of knowing for certain. One thing we do know – however miraculous childbirth may be, it is also very messy. God did not arrive in a more sanitary way than anyone else – His birth was real. Many tellings of the story imagine Joseph assisting at the birth, or Mary alone. I imagine it is likely that Joseph would have sought out more experienced help as there's nothing to suggest the arrival of the baby happened within moments of them arriving in the town.

Ponder

What do you need to feel 'at home' somewhere? Why do you think God chose such a squalid place for His Son to be born?

Pray

Pray for those who are facing adverse living conditions this winter due to poverty, displacement or war.

God our shepherd

Opening prayer

Present God, You are our shepherd. Thank You for guiding us and providing what we need. Amen.

Bible reading

Luke 2:8–14

From Gabriel's perspective

This just gets better and better. Shepherds! Probably no one's first guess at God's favoured ones but bang on the money! Well, lack of money. If you're going to give a front row seat to someone, it should be them. The ones who are always at the back of the queue but spend their lives doing the daily grind of caring for others. Caring for others who are often stubborn, stupid and a bit stinky. So we gave them a glimpse of glory! Well, they deserve it! It was just a tiny glimpse of heavenly praise and worship, with a blessing of peace. Although before all of that I made sure to give them the address they needed to go and check it out.

I'm so excited! We all are! I thought we sang particularly well because of that. We were quite loud as well. Probably why we scared them. Oops. Oh well, a healthy amount of fear will jimmy them along. And, of course, the good news of great joy for everyone that they definitely don't want to miss out on!

Shepherds off to see the great shepherd. Poetic.

Luke specifies that Gabriel went to visit Zechariah and Mary. This passage talks of an 'angel of the Lord' without name, who is joined by 'the great company of a heavenly host'. We don't know for sure whether it was Gabriel or not because he didn't introduce himself to the shepherds who recounted the story. But I've always imagined that it was Gabriel, seeing as he seems to be chief messenger on this subject and seems to know what's going on!

Shepherds are not unusual in the Scriptures, literally and metaphorically. The patriarchs are shepherds – Abraham, Isaac, Jacob, Joseph and his brothers, Moses too. Numbers 14:33 tells us that the Hebrews are shepherds in the wilderness for 40 years. The children of Israel are often described as sheep without a shepherd and we hear how God longs to be their shepherd if they will follow. Jacob talks of 'the God who has been my shepherd all my life to this day' (Gen. 48:15). King David famously writes, 'The LORD is my shepherd' in Psalm 23, and Isaiah 40:11 talks of the Lord shepherding His people. The major and minor prophets are full of warnings about false shepherds and the punishment they will receive for leading people astray.

Of course, many of the mentions of shepherds come from Jesus – but at that first Christmas, they didn't know what He was going to say – principally, 'I am the good shepherd… [who] lays down his life for the sheep' (John 10:11). So it's not really a surprise that shepherds get to be the first visitors to God on earth – they are clearly some of his favourites for all that they represent about the heart of God and His care for His people. Jesus comes as *the* shepherd so that all may follow Him to the Father.

Ponder
Are you shepherding anyone? Who needs your care, attention and protection?

Pray
Pray for those you know who are seeking guidance, that they would find wise counsel.

DAY 16

God our Saviour

Opening prayer

Present God, if You hadn't been born as a person, You couldn't have saved us in the way You did. Thank You, Jesus. Amen.

Bible reading

Luke 2:15–20

From a shepherd's perspective

The lambs we watch are important. We don't look after them for any normal uses. No shearing for wool, no breeding, no milking for cheese. These are kept young and healthy, without blemish, ready for sacrifice. Probably killed too young if we listened to what they wanted.

It may not be glamourous work, but it has significance. These animals atone for the sins of all Israel, so I do wish the public at large would show a bit more gratitude. But someone noticed. God noticed.

It was pretty awesome to be honest. I've seen plenty of shooting stars but I reckon the angels were better. I wasn't scared.

Alright, I was a bit scared, but I think you'll forgive me...

So we had to go. Straight away. No dilly-dallying. No shilly-shallying. When God calls you to see something, you run to see it. So we did. We were in on the moment when God did something brilliant!

What the angel said was right and we know that God has let us in on something special. We've been telling everyone we meet. Some old guy told me that Bethlehem is where Israel's sovereign ruler is going to come from, and that the Scriptures say that he'll feed his flock! So if he's finally here then we get to be the sheep for a change. But I wonder who gets sacrificed? I'll think about that later. If he's the shepherd, then he can do the worrying.

Alfred Edersheim, a Jewish man who came to beleive in Jesus, wrote a book called *The Life and Times of Jesus the Messiah* in 1883. He made the interesting observation that the Mishnah (from ancient Jewish writings) suggested a common belief that the Messiah would be revealed from 'the tower of the flock'. This tower stood close to Bethlehem on the road to Jerusalem. The sheep that pastured there were not the type used for ordinary purposes but temple-flocks meant for sacrifice. He went on to surmise that those watching the sheep meant for slaughter are the first to receive the message about the ultimate Lamb who would take away the sins of the world. The shepherds we read about in Luke's Gospel obviously weren't aware of the death and resurrection of Jesus that would come thirty or so years later, but for those of us who can piece together the puzzle in retrospect, it's an interesting point to consider.

On Day 4 we looked at Micah 5:2–4, where we heard the birthplace of the Messiah prophesied. In verse 4, it references the shepherd-role of Jesus as He feeds His flock, so I like the idea of the shepherds who visited Him as a baby hearing those words. In our industrialised world, shepherding is not regularly used as a metaphor, but the benefit of hindsight and biblical knowledge gives us insight into how the story fits together and the importance of this occupation for God.

Ponder
The shepherds drop everything to go and see Jesus. Is there anything you need to let go of so you can pursue Him more purposefully?

Pray
Pray for those who may be overlooked, perhaps while caring for others, that they would feel valued and know the message of Jesus this Christmas.

SESSION THREE

Repercussion

DAY 17

Forgiveness made possible

Opening prayer

Compassionate God, You see all our imperfections. Please make us right before You. Amen.

Bible reading

Malachi 3:1–6

From Simeon's perspective

I long to give an offering to the Lord that pleases him. Presenting an offering in righteousness has been my life's goal. I haven't figured out a way to put myself in a fire and come out cleaner. It may work for silver and gold but I would be charred at best. The only way will be by the anointed one. How will he do it? I don't know exactly. He'll make an offering, a sacrifice more holy than we are able to make, a perfect one. He will know how.

I am longing for him to come and yet I fear because I know he will. There will be such joy when he arrives for he will help us turn to God – but judgment will be far from celebratory. None can escape because none are sinless. We cling to the promise that our returning is mutual. God will return to us as we return to him.

There are repercussions to the coming of Jesus. These, like expectation, can be both good and bad. He comes quietly, unnoticed by most, but His presence cannot be missed, particularly in the big picture. He cannot come and make no impact. In this third session, we'll consider some of the effects of His coming.

Malachi is the final book of the Old Testament and many think he was the last of the prophets. He was writing about 400 years before the birth of Jesus so, following this, there was a very long silence from

God. I have used Simeon, again, to ponder these words. (We'll come to his own passage soon!)

If this Scripture had been used to speak of the coming Messiah – a refiner's fire, a fuller's soap – then no wonder Herod and all Jerusalem were scared, as we'll see over the next few days. A fuller is someone who removes oil, dirt and impurities from wool, and the process involves stretching, beating and scouring. Being cleansed doesn't sound like a fun process, and, in today's reading, Malachi asks who will be able to endure it. It's a poetic way of saying no one is worthy of standing before God, or indeed Jesus (here called the Lord of Hosts and the Messenger of the Covenant, respectively). Verse 5 talks of judgment, then verse 6 offers hope. At this stage it is unknown how the cleansing will occur, but the anointed one will purify His people so that what they offer to the Lord will please Him.

Reading the whole context of Malachi, the offerings that will please God are as follows: our love for Him, our honour and respect by giving our best rather than our leftovers or what we have stolen, our faithfulness, honesty and right-living, and our generosity. Certainly the earthly life of Jesus and His teaching can help us with all of those things.

Ponder
In recent days or weeks, what things have you thought, said or done that would not have pleased God?

Pray
Thank Jesus for coming to wash our wrongdoings away, and ask for His help in living a life pleasing to God.

DAY 18

Heaven opened to all

Opening prayer

Compassionate God, thank You for Jesus' promise of 'seek and you will find'. Thank You that He can be found by all, regardless of race, religion, education or location. Amen.

Bible reading

Matthew 2:1–2

From one of the magi's perspective

What made us set off? I don't know. A thirst for adventure. A longing for knowledge. A deep conviction that this particular alignment of planets must mean the birth of a regal power.

We felt the King of the Judeans would be a king worth knowing about, whatever your faith or religion. A Messiah would certainly be of interest regardless of your persuasion. I worship the all-wise god, but he doesn't dwell here with us. If he were to send an envoy, it would change everything. The unusual combination of stars certainly seemed to suggest something along those lines.

We didn't all go. Just those of us who were most keen. I think it would be fair to say it was those of us who most felt that we still hadn't found what we'd spent so many years looking for, that there was a piece of our puzzle missing. What did we have to lose? We headed in the direction suggested by the sky, and asked for the palace when we got close.

We felt a rising excitement with every day that passed. We may have been tired, but our pilgrimage was filled with hope about who we would find beneath the 'X' on the heavenly treasure map.

The Greek word 'magi' *magos* has been variously understood to mean sages, priests or astronomers. It is generally accepted that they be called 'wise' due to their keen study of religion, natural sciences and the mysteries of the universe. Some suggest their origin, called 'the east', refers to Babylon, which in biblical times was most associated with their kind of study. Putting these things together, it's a strong possibility that they might have been Zoroastrian priests. Their god is known as 'Wise Lord', which may be where they got their name. There is nothing to suggest there were three of them, only the three gifts they brought with them.

It is interesting that it is 'outsiders' who first come seeking Jesus. There are many in Israel who understand that the Messiah is to be born in Bethlehem, but despite the rumours, the story of the shepherds, the visit of the magi, none of them go looking. None that we hear of are intrigued enough even to travel a short distance out of curiosity.

The magi travel a long distance, certain that the newborn King is worthy of homage. It proves that God's grace is not limited to those within certain countries or tribes, or to those within 'reach', but that He can draw people to Himself by any means He chooses. He will certainly be found by those who are looking. In this case, He uses a star (or celestial light) to guide them. The explanations about what kind of light it could have been are far too lengthy for discussion here. Suffice to say that many believe genuine guidance of the astronomical kind is the most likely explanation. God, who made the universe, can do anything after all.

Ponder

What led you to Jesus? Were you looking for Him?

Pray

Pray for those who are spiritually searching – that Jesus would meet them right where they are.

DAY 19

A new kingdom

Opening prayer

Compassionate God, thank You for the kingdom of heaven that Jesus has established. May we welcome it into our lives. Amen.

Bible reading

Matthew 2:3–8

From Herod's perspective

Visits from foreign dignitaries are one of my favourite things. If people want to travel from afar to pay homage to me then they're welcome.

Thirty-five years, I've been ruling. They don't call me 'the Great' for no reason. Turning up at my palace with gifts for someone else is rude. It's my land. It's my time. If anyone presents a challenge to my authority then I must do something. What kingdom is available for a rival?

One opinion was not enough, so I called all the priests and scribes. Annoyingly they all agreed with no hesitation and without conferring. The Christ was to be born in Bethlehem, not far away. Even worse, a couple of cocky ones pointed out that the calculations for dates as prophesied by Daniel meant that the arrival was imminent too.

I'm not ready to let go yet. I'm sure my people don't want unnecessary change either. I need to protect them. I'll speak to the visitors in private. No need for undue alarm. A plan is unfolding in my mind.

The word the magi use, which most Bibles translate as 'worship' or 'homage', is *proskunesai*. It means to fawn, crouch or prostrate oneself to adore. It can suggest 'to kiss', like a dog licking the hand. I imagine all of these things were what Herod the Great would like done to him, yet here are guests seeking to pay that devotion to another. We are told that Herod's response is fear. It could be fear of a rival, fear of his own mortality, fear of his sin, or fear of losing power in his own kingdom. I find it strange that in today's passage Matthew adds, 'and all Jerusalem with him'. Is it that when Herod is scared, the whole city is scared? In *Matthew Henry's Complete Commentary on the Whole Bible* it suggests their fear could be of war in a troubled region or fear of having to adjust their own behavior when salvation comes. He cites their mistaken belief that the kingdom of the Messiah would clash with secular powers as their key concern. Throughout the Gospels, we hear Jesus talk of His kingdom and we learn that it isn't an earthly territory, although many at the time were expecting that from the Messiah.

As we saw briefly on Day 4, Bethlehem means 'bread house'. In addition, there was a famous well there. King David (who was from Bethlehem) talks of a longing to drink from it (2 Sam. 23:15). The Messiah, who will shepherd His people, arrives in a place known for the provision of bread and water. There are so many things in the story of His birth that express the 'spiritual' leadership of Jesus. At the time, the people were still blind, perhaps unwilling to see, what His birth was for and what kind of eternal kingdom would be established.

Ponder

Do you find it easy to relinquish any power you might have? How can we allow Jesus to lead us, rather than trying to control things for ourselves?

Pray

Pray that the kingdom of heaven would be near to those who are fearful, or living under threat or terror.

DAY 20

A worldwide family

Opening prayer

Compassionate God, help us to listen and learn from others, and to extend Your welcome to all. Amen.

Bible reading

Matthew 2:9–12

From one of the Magi's perspective

We were welcomed at the palace, but something felt strange. Certainly it was not the location of the king we sought. Their scholars knew where we should look and I was surprised they did not join our quest. It was soon to become clear it was their loss.

When we arrived at the right place, we were filled with joy all over and under, and danced with joy both inside and out. Rejoicing seemed to have been born in us like the child was born in Bethlehem! We bowed to him and presented gifts that we had brought from our land. Our journey was not in vain – we found what we were looking for, and our celestial nudge had been correct. It will prove to be a life-changing encounter for all of us.

That night, several of us had concurring dreams about the king from the palace. We knew we must avoid him and not reveal the child's location. The wailing of distraught mothers that echoed in our sleep made us sure worship was not his intent. We felt some sadness there, for those being so near and yet still so far. Despite that, our joy continued to bubble inside and boil over for our journey home, as we imagined the faces of those we would tell on our return.

In the NRSV, verse 10 of today's reading says the magi 'were overwhelmed with joy'. In the KJV it says, 'they rejoiced with exceeding great joy'. I think the latter might be closer to the original. The Greek seems to say something along the lines of, 'they were joyed (rejoiced) with great vehement joy'. 'Vehement' comes from an uncertain derivation but can be used for violent, as well as exceeding, great or in high degree. It paints a lively picture of some very excited people!

The magi bring gifts as foreign dignitaries would, and as an act of worship. It has been suggested that the gifts signify the identity of Christ: gold because He is King, frankincense (a worship offering) because He is God, and myrrh (often used for embalming) because He is human.

As we saw a few days ago, the magi were neither Jewish nor local, and yet were among the first to bow in worship. The arrival of Jesus opens God's family to all. Thus far the children of Israel, in differing collections, have been carrying the faith for thousands of years. These early visitors to Jesus signify, right from the beginning, that all are welcome, and worshipping Him will not be solely for the Jews. Finding Jesus will be open to anyone who is looking. He will be found in different ways that are suitable to the seeker.

Matthew Henry's commentary on the Bible points out that Gentiles knew the time of Jesus' birth by the stars, and Jews knew the place from the Scriptures. He suggests, therefore, that we all have something to learn from each other, and if we communicate with others, it will result in an increase of knowledge for all.

Ponder
From what background did you come to find Jesus? Is the same true for your family or friends?

Pray
Pray for those you know, or in your community, who practice other religions.

DAY 21

An eternal home

Opening prayer

Compassionate God, thank You for our eternal home. Please journey with us through life until then. Amen.

Bible reading

Matthew 2:13–15

From Joseph's perspective

Another angelic visitation. I'm starting to get used to these...

It's nice to know we get a heads-up when danger is coming our way. It will make being an earthly father to the Son of God a little easier. Maybe. Although there was nothing easy about fleeing to Egypt and I doubt there'll be anything easy about our life here until Herod is gone.

We left the instant my dream woke me. Not worth risking another moment. We travelled by night, and took nothing with us to slow us down. Travelling with a toddler is hard enough in the daylight with a caravan, let alone with neither. But it's his life that's worth saving beyond anything else, and that is why we're here.

I will have to find work. Odd jobs until something sticks. I've no idea how long we'll need to stay and what sort of accommodation I should look for. No idea where to start looking in a country we don't know.

No ideas. That seems to be the theme. Maybe the angel will turn up again with some helpful words if I fall asleep. Right now I feel like I could sleep standing up and for a week! But I can't. I have to protect this little band of nomads and try to make us a home on the run.

One of the repercussions of Jesus coming is that He can invite us to an eternal (and permanent) home. John 3:16 is well known in describing why Jesus came to earth: 'For God so loved the world that he gave his one and only son, that whoever believes in him shall not perish but have eternal life.' This promised eternal life will be in the new heaven and new earth that we read about in Revelation 21 and 22. We can live there with God because Jesus has reconciled us to Him. We may not have the luxury of permanence in this life, or even safety to stay in one place, but we have hope for a home with God in the future because of His Son.

Jesus knows what it is to be nomadic – He lived in Bethlehem, Egypt and Nazareth before He was ten years old. When His ministry began, He continued this travelling lifestyle and said, 'the Son of Man has nowhere to lay His head' (Matt. 8:20).

I think there is a special place in the heart of Jesus for those who experience homelessness or displacement. His time spent in Egypt is as an asylum seeker. Joseph had to flee there with his family to avoid those who would seek to destroy the newly arrived Saviour. When people leave their homes and travel hundreds of miles, often through fierce danger, they are seeking safety, security, a better life and a brighter future for their children. The only way we can hope for a better life beyond this world is through Jesus.

Ponder

Do you ever think about eternal life? What do you think it might be like?

Pray

Pray for the many refugees in our world, whether internally displaced or in foreign lands.

DAY 22

Sorrow in this life

Opening prayer

Compassionate God, thank You that You are with us in our time of need. Be our comforter in painful times. Amen.

Bible reading

Matthew 2:16–18

From Rachel's perspective

My son. My sweet baby boy with his soft, smooth skin and chubby cheeks. He is gone. He is gone and my heart has gone with him.

I feel numb now. For weeks I have yelled and screamed and sobbed until my face was raw and my voice was gone. Now I am silent. I have buried myself with my lost boy. He was taken before he had time to become who he was meant to be.

Who were they looking for? What threat did he pose? What baby could be so dangerous as to warrant this corporate sentence? A coward takes a child before he's grown into an adversary. I wonder if they found him. I wonder, did it work, whatever this was meant to achieve? What death could ever bring a greater good?

God is judge. That can be my only comfort. When people try to deal out judgment, no one wins. And Israel weeps again.

Why is it our lot to lose so much and so often? Where is our anointed one to restore our future? He will bring justice, but who knows when? How near are the promises of God? I wish I could reach out and touch them. I wish for so much.

The first Rachel was the wife of Jacob, who was also known as 'Israel'; therefore she is a representative of all Israelites. She is the mother of Joseph (in the Old Testament, not the man who raised

Jesus!), and we read that she died in childbirth with her second son, Benjamin (Gen. 35:18).

It is hard to put words to the 'great mourning' (or 'loud lamentation', NRSV) of someone who refuses to be consoled (v18). There were probably few words used. I imagine this is the least 'festive' of readings for the Christmas period. Herod has all the young children around Bethlehem killed. It is a brutal repercussion of the arrival of Jesus, fuelled by the fear of a threatened ruler. With those gathered for the census it is a desperate loss for one tribe. Being a small village, educated guesses calculate the number murdered at around 25. The Greek word used for those slaughtered could be translated 'boys' or 'children'. Many translations opt for the latter, showing the significance of a universal attack on Israel. Other translations choose to specify that boys were killed, echoing the massacre of Jewish baby boys by the Egyptians in Exodus 1 and 2.

The quote about Rachel in this passage is taken from Jeremiah 31. In its original context, it is sandwiched in between the joy of God calling Israel's exiles home and the promise that He will establish a new covenant with them. Matthew specifically draws our attention to the fact that Jesus' birth is the start of these promises being fulfilled, but he knows there is still heartache. There will always be heartache until every tear is wiped away as promised in Revelation 21:4, which is to be after the second coming of Jesus, rather than the first.

Ponder

Have you ever known life to be 'bittersweet'? Where have you seen joy and heartache side by side? Could you see God at work there?

Pray

Pray for those you know suffering with grief, or loneliness, particularly at this time of year. Ask God to show you who you can reach out to.

DAY 23

Nowhere forgotten

Opening prayer
Compassionate God, You care about the forgotten and unloved places. Help us to care for them too. Amen.

Bible reading
Matthew 2:19–23

From Gabriel's perspective
Poor Joseph. Me again, haunting his dreams. Twice more. I hope I'll be leaving them in peace for a while.

I think Egypt has been what they call 'an experience'. Nice to be able to tell them to head home. Home to the backwater. I've heard this joke, 'Three Nazarenes walk into a bar...' Actually, I won't tell it. No need to reinforce stereotypes that may or may not be true. Learn to button it, Gabe.

Best to avoid Jerusalem, anyway. Safer out of the spotlight. They can always visit. There'll be plenty of fun to be had around Galilee somewhere, I'm sure. So, this is when life gets normal. For a while, at least. As normal as it can be. In fact, yes, completely normal. Nothing to write home about. Jesus will hang out in Nowheresville until he's ready and decides it's time to be noticed again. Can't wait!

Luke 2:39 says that after everything had been done as required by the law, the family went home to Nazareth. Some think of it as a contradiction with this story and the flight to Egypt described in Matthew's narrative. However, neither gives a specific timescale, so it's perfectly possible that both are true, depending on how you work out timings and what order things happened. Very learned historians don't seem to be able to agree on exactly when Herod died and how long a census would take, so the dating of Jesus' birth and the events around it is tricky.

The telling of these dreams makes Joseph seem so very obedient and fast-acting. The angel says, 'get up' – so Joseph 'gets up'. I wonder whether there is any time lapse between those actions! The flight to Egypt was likely to have been immediate if they sensed Jesus was in danger. Returning to Israel may have been a more leisurely affair.

Herod Archelaus was the son of Herod the Great and had succeeded the throne. It seemed safer to avoid him, just in case. So they chose to go home to Nazareth, rather than settling nearer to the centre of things. Again, it fulfills prophecy from the Old Testament Scriptures, and the Gospel writers make sure we understand that Jesus is the one who fulfills the new covenant in every possible way. He is described as 'Jesus of Nazareth' throughout the Gospels, and everyone seems to have completely forgotten (or chosen to blot out) the details of his extraordinary birth. Nazareth adds to the low-key profile that Jesus arrives with. We hear the joke, 'Nazareth! Can anything good come from there?' (John 1:46). Similar to Bethlehem, I think it shows us God's special love for those avoided by others. There are places that people write off – inaccessible rural spots, estates where no one wants to live – but God loves them, and chooses to dwell there. He sees those that feel ignored or forgotten, and He is at home with them.

Ponder

Where do you think Jesus might be born and grow up if He were to come (for the first time) today?

Pray

Pray for the areas in your community that are considered to be deprived or dangerous.

DAY 24

Unassailable peace

Opening prayer

Compassionate God, thank You that You have conquered evil. May we know Your peace in our lives and in our world. Amen.

Bible reading

Luke 1:57–80

From Zechariah's perspective

There may have been no John in this family until now, but we will not argue with the name the Lord has chosen for the gift he has given us. Besides, 'God is gracious' is a name to which we can say 'Amen!' with the greatest conviction. As soon as I confirmed it, my tongue was free and I could speak again. The words that came tumbling out were the things I had been thinking of and saving up for nine months – words of praise and knowledge about our standout son and his saving cousin.

God's favour, of course, is where I began. It is where we all begin. How could we not? In John's childhood we will see so much more of it, I know. And when the time comes for him to go before the Lord, to prepare the way for the anointed one, my heart will burst for love of God and for my son. Change is coming and he must herald it.

We have known such oppression and hardship. We live under foreign rule once again. People seem so quick to pick a fight. The evil one is hard at work. Yet with these boys comes the time for God to rise up against it. Israel will no longer be the victim! Judeans will no longer be slaves to sin or to anyone else! All of our enemies, within and without, even the evil one, will be silenced.

Listen to me! It's no wonder people think I'm a crazy old fool!

The words in Zechariah's prophecy sum up all the content we have seen in this Christmas story: a new covenant promised; promises mercifully remembered; the coming of a Saviour; light in the darkness; forgiveness of sins; serving without fear. In addition, there is a double mention here of being rescued from enemies (vv71,73). The word for enemy can mean hateful or odious people. It can be used of hostile or opposing people. It can refer to humankind as enemies of God by our sin. And it is used to reference Satan as the ultimate enemy. So in the coming of Jesus, those who are hateful will be conquered, those who are hostile will be silenced, those who are sinful will be freed and Satan will be trampled. An all-round trouncing of enemies, I would say!

One of the biggest repercussions of Jesus coming to earth is the ultimate conquering of evil, including its ringleader. As a result of that, Zechariah concludes with peace. The Greek word for peace, *eirene,* as with *shalom* in Hebrew, seems to include wholeness (being set at one) and prosperity, along with the personal and corporate quiet and rest of which we might first think. If Satan and earthly enemies are silenced, then there certainly will be peace, both for nations and individuals.

Ponder
How can you know the peace of God despite the presence of those who oppose it?

Pray
Pray for peace today – within your family, your community, and across the world.

SESSION FOUR

Reverberation

Direct access

Opening prayer

Mighty God, we praise You that You know us and we can know You.
May we live by Your law in our hearts. Amen.

Bible reading

Jeremiah 31:31–34

Today's Bible reading is an amazing piece of Scripture. It's a passage
that gives me goosebumps: 'they will all know me, from the least of
them to the greatest' (v34). In this instance, I don't want to put more
words in Jeremiah's mouth, or indeed God's. Why not read these
verses again?

The reverberations of Christ's coming are manifold. Life on earth
will never be the same; the ripples will be felt across all people and
generations for eternity. His coming reverberates every time someone
encounters and decides to follow Him.

The coming of Jesus marks the switch from the Old Testament to
the New. It is the move from God's first covenant with His people
to what is called the new covenant. 'Covenant' means a solemn
agreement or contractual pledge. Biblically, it's often thought of as a
promise. The metaphor of a marriage between God and His people is
repeatedly used throughout the Bible.

If you'll allow me to over-simplify, I think it can be useful to explore
the coming of Jesus by summing up the early parts of the Bible: God
promises to be with His people, and gives them His law to help them
to honour Him and to look after each other. The law is written on
stone tablets and stored in the Ark in the Tabernacle or Temple. The
people continue to be unfaithful to Him by ignoring the law and doing
their own thing. The prophets warn them of the impact of this, so they

repent and return. This repeats many times. The prophets also keep hope alive with the promise of a new covenant that will make being faithful to God a whole lot more accessible… it will be in the shape of a Saviour.

Jeremiah explains that when the new covenant is made (when the Saviour comes), there won't be the same need for loud-mouthed prophets or representatives, like Moses, to speak to the Lord on behalf of the people. Everyone will be able to speak to God and hear from Him directly. It's by far the biggest impact of the coming of Jesus that evangelicals talk about – everyone can have a personal relationship with God because of Jesus.

This does not mean that the law has become obsolete. In His sermon on the mount, Jesus says that He has not come to abolish the law, but to fulfill it (Matt. 5:17). It remains important to live by the standards God has set. But there is now a key difference. In Romans and Hebrews, Paul echoes the words from Jeremiah that in the new covenant (after the coming of Jesus) God's law is no longer written in stone, but is written on our hearts. We won't necessarily know everything instinctively, but by investing in our relationship with God, by reading the Bible, through talking and listening to Him, through praise, through discussion with others, our consciences will become attuned to His desires.

Ponder

Do you ever think of God's law as being written on your heart? Could it be a helpful image for you?

Pray

Pray for someone you know who doesn't yet have a personal relationship with God through Jesus.

DAY 26
No fear

Opening prayer
Mighty God, You have given us freedom and choice. We choose to follow Jesus today. Amen.

Bible reading
Luke 2:22–35

From Simeon's perspective
Bury me a happy man! I have lived long enough and I have seen God's rescue plan! Today was enough for me. My lifetime ambition fulfilled. I held him in my arms – my frail arms, strengthened with joy – I held the one who comes to save! I cannot fear death now.

I blessed his parents and prayed for them. Such an honour! I didn't want to tell them they'll need it, but I had to. Perhaps it will help when they remember it. His mother is strong but she loves so much; she will be cut to the heart by how he is treated.

And what about the rest of us? I think this may be a test, a marker. It will expose what is in hearts and minds; it will show where loyalties lie; it will reveal priorities. How each responds to this will be their making. There will be choice. There is always choice. And praise God there is grace. So much grace…

Simeon demonstrates that there need be no fear of death for those in Christ. That is a life-changing reverberation of Jesus coming. Death, often thought of as an enemy, holds no power anymore. 1 Corinthians 15 considers the impact of this, culminating with, 'Where, O death, is your victory? Where, O death, is your sting?' (1 Cor. 15:55).

Simeon is 'righteous and devout' and looking forward to the coming

Messiah (v25). This is probably why the Holy Spirit rests on him! He has been told by the Spirit that he won't die until he has seen the anointed one. On this particular day, at just the right moment, he is led by the Spirit to the temple. Mary and Joseph have brought Jesus for dedication. They offer two turtle doves as thanksgiving for their firstborn, an offering allowed for those who can't afford a larger animal. Because Simeon takes Jesus in his arms, and blesses the parents, it is thought he could be the priest carrying out the dedication. His actions must be more confirmation of Jesus' identity for his parents (if they needed it).

Simeon speaks of how the arrival of Jesus will have an effect across people groups, His light bringing revelation and glory. Simeon speaks specifically of Israel when he says that Jesus will reveal people's inner thoughts and cause 'the falling and rising of many' (v34). He warns Mary that Jesus will be opposed, and that there will be piercing sadness ahead for her.

The phrase about revealing inner thoughts made me think about our human nature and our natural desires. We are made with free will and will never be forced to accept that Jesus is the Messiah. He will not enter where He is not wanted. He will know those inner thoughts, whatever they are, and respond accordingly.

Ponder

When and how did you first choose to follow Jesus? Has it been something you have re-decided regularly?

Pray

Pray that all would have an opportunity to hear the news of Jesus and respond freely.

DAY 27

Open ears

Opening prayer

Mighty God, may we be open to hearing from You and seeing You at work. Amen.

Bible reading

Luke 2:36–38

From Anna's perspective

The redemption of Jerusalem can be a hot topic around here. The when and the how, mostly. I've kept my mouth shut. Sixty years I have prayed, fasted, worshipped and kept quiet. But not today. Today, I got gobby.

'If you're looking for the answer to all your expectations, he's here!' I shouted.

How did I know? I can't explain it, I just did. I knew it in my knower. I'm not sure if that's my head, my heart or my gut. Probably all three.

Not everyone is looking. They may know that God has promised salvation for Israel, but they're not necessarily looking for it. Anyone who is looking will hear from me from now on. I will go on telling. If people want to know, then there's someone to watch. I would have continued praising to my death had I not seen him, for what else is there to do? But now I worship with renewed energy, passion and excitement. Redemption is on its way. It will not come like a flood because not everyone is ready. It will be like a slow trickle, noticed by those with eyes to see and ears to hear, accepted by those whose hearts are open, life-changing for those who are willing to follow. If it weren't for my arthritis I would dance! Oh what the heck, I'll dance anyway and put up with the indigestion!

God is coming with a slow creep to save all who will be saved.

But some won't see it. They're not willing to trust whatever comes next and be surprised by his plan. I like a surprise. I don't even care about the effect on my heart. I have seen the Messiah and my heart is full enough for anything.

This passage says that Anna began to praise God and to speak about the child (v38). The word used for 'speak' is described by *Strong's Exhaustive Concordance of the Bible* as a 'prolonged form of an otherwise obsolete verb'. It means to talk, but not so much a one-off sermon as a seriously extended going-off-on-one! It implies that Anna continues talking incessantly about the child to 'all who are looking for the redemption of Jerusalem'. In this sentence, 'looking for' can be translated 'anticipating', or the literal sense seems to be 'the ones open to receiving'.

I hope I am open to receiving. I want to see the reverberations caused by the coming of Christ around me all the time. I guess I need my ears and eyes open to the Spirit for Him to reveal it to me. God is at work and we can easily miss it. It is worth noting that Anna chooses her audience. She doesn't yell at everyone, she talks to those who are open. It is a good lesson in timely evangelism.

Ponder

When do you feel you last saw God at work in someone's life, or your own? Do you look for it?

Pray

Pray for someone, perhaps yourself, who you would like to be more open to being surprised by God.

Growing understanding

Opening prayer

Mighty God, give us more understanding of You with each year that passes. Amen.

Bible reading

Luke 2:41–52

From Mary's perspective

I'll be telling the story of that trip for years – the year we lost him in the capital city for three days! It will never leave my mind.

I've never completely relaxed into thinking that I've got motherhood nailed. I fail too often. That was a particularly spectacular fail for me, and yet he was cool as a cucumber and saw nothing out of the ordinary about those few days at all. I wanted to box him around the ears except I couldn't stop kissing him. My heart has never raced so fast for so long! I apologised to the priests and teachers but they seemed sad to see him go.

He's never caused us any bother on purpose. In fact, he's been an absolute dream. His cheekiness leans on the funny side. But there are moments when his head is in the clouds – he gets so deep into a thought or conversation that he completely forgets about normal things like eating or coming home. But I wouldn't change him. As if I could.

I love thinking of the community of travellers together – they make the pilgrimage to Jerusalem regularly for festivals and know each other well. It takes a whole day for Mary and Joseph to realise that Jesus isn't with them, such is their trust in the crowd. It then takes three days before they finally track Him down in the Temple. He is asking, listening, understanding and answering. The three day conversation must have been fascinating enough for the teachers not to dismiss a 12-year-old boy.

Jesus goes on to have discussions of this kind throughout his ministry – many ask Him questions and He often replies with more questions. The Jewish faith is known to be discursive – believers are encouraged to discuss the Scriptures and thrash out meaning and understanding in the process. In its good moments, Christianity is similarly open to challenge and deep thinking through discourse. A clear reverberation from the coming of Jesus is how widely talked about He is. There are many opinions; even the synoptic Gospels differ slightly in their accounts. But Jesus wasn't scared of an argument and welcomed a debate.

They say that the older you get, the more you realise how little you know. But this in itself is a kind of wisdom! This passage finishes by saying that Jesus increased in wisdom as well as in years (or 'stature', depending on your translation). He also increased in favour with God and people. A very clever teenage boy would be unlikely to be popular, unless he was also wise in when and how he shared it! Being cocky would not have made Him very likeable; He must've been good at listening too. His understanding included understanding of people as well as theology – except when He tells his mother that His whereabouts was obvious and she should've known. But then all boys wind their mothers up, and He was fully human after all…

Ponder

What are the things you don't understand about faith that you'd like to discuss with someone?

Pray

Pray for children and young people you know, that they would grow to know more of God.

Empowered life

Opening prayer

Mighty God, we acknowledge our need for You. Thank You for the empowering of Your Spirit. Amen.

Bible reading

Matthew 3:1–12 or Luke 3:1–20

From John the Baptist's perspective

Preparing a straight path for the Lord is my tunnel vision. A lifetime's commitment. People think me strange, but I prefer to call it 'focused'.

The path for the Lord is a two-way street. The people must be ready to receive and the Lord must have clear access to give. For this to happen, all must understand their need to repent because we have failed the Lord. We need not beat ourselves up about it, we are only human after all, but we must at least know that we need his help. It's simple, really.

Being a descendent of Abraham won't buy you any more favour than anyone else. There aren't any magic words, secret handshakes or free passes. We only need to know that we need him. I've always said that God could raise up stones to follow him if the people won't. He doesn't need us. But he likes us. Strange but true. And the anointed one can douse us in the Spirit to give us the very best chance of bearing good fruit and avoiding the agony of separation from him. So who's next?

Full immersion in water was part of the Hebrew tradition for certain purification rites. Among other occasions, it was required when converting to the faith and on the day before holy festivals. It was not unusual for John to suggest baptism for repentance, but he is certainly giving a fresh challenge about the motivation for it. He is clear to point out to the Pharisees and Sadducees that they must 'produce fruit in keeping with repentance' rather than just carrying out a ritual. He is asking for a heart change, as following Jesus will require more than going through the motions. We prepare for meeting with Jesus by confessing our sins – He is able to judge between wheat and chaff and we need to know our need of Him.

John goes on to promise a new baptism with the fire of the Holy Spirit which, he says, comes with the arrival of Jesus. The Spirit has always been present and empowering, but He will now be more freely and readily available because we are made worthy of His presence by Jesus. In addition, Jesus later tells us that He has to go to heaven in order that the Spirit can fully come (John 16:7), which He does at Pentecost (Acts 2).

Jesus tells Nicodemus that 'no one can enter the kingdom of God without being born of water and Spirit' (John 3:5). Through Jesus, baptism becomes a key turning point for believers – the sinful self is put to death and it marks the start of a new life in Christ. It need not be done more than once (even though we are continually repenting of sin) – the rebirth has happened and the new life has begun. We are also baptised in the fire of the Spirit for the empowering to live a life more like Jesus.

Ponder

When do you feel you are 'going through the motions' of faith, and when do you feel that your heart is engaged?

Pray

Pray that the Christian life for you, and those you know, will be more than 'going through the motions'.

Perfect unity

Opening prayer

Mighty God, thank You for modelling perfect community. Amen.

Bible reading

Matthew 3:13–17 or Luke 3:21–22

From Gabriel's perspective

I think this moment may be my favourite of all moments. To be honest, I've got a lot of favourite moments. It's so hard to choose when you've witnessed them all! But there was something particularly special about having them all in the same place together, in the earthly space where John was doing his important work. Jesus, the human contingent, saying he was ready to get cracking. The Spirit descending as a dove and the Father booming his big, chuffed voice out about his Son so everyone could definitely hear it. I was practically jumping up and down.

The humans don't usually get to see all three of them at the same time. I think they find it quite hard to get their heads around God, but it's really quite simple when you live with them. 'Hear, O Israel: the LORD our God, the LORD is one.' Three persons, yes, but one God. They discuss things, then they always agree, so they've no need to go their own way. Unlike human beings...

I don't know if I've picked it up from the Bible (perhaps Heb. 12:1) or if it is purely my imagination, but I like to think of heavenly 'witnesses' watching what is happening on earth. I imagine at this point that, with all his important involvement thus far, Gabriel wants to know how things are unfolding. So, just for fun, I've set him up as an audience member of Jesus' baptism.

The coming of Jesus helps us to understand the Trinity – a key reverberation. The word used for God in the Old Testament (*Elohim*) is a plural form of the noun, even though He is referred to as one God. Gabriel (in today's imagined spoken piece) quotes Deuteronomy 6:4, which is prayed daily in Judaism. All three members of the Trinity are certainly mentioned in their individual roles throughout the Old Testament. In the New Testament, however, there is much more clarity about the three and how they work together. Jesus' baptism is one of very few Bible passages where all three are mentioned at once, and I think the only time when all three are experienced in a palpable way by those present.

We can often get tied in knots about the Trinity, but, put as simply as I can, I understand it like this: the Father, the Son and the Spirit are all distinct persons; they are all eternal; they all exist at once; they relate to each other; they are all fully God; they are all the same God. I think this shows us that in the same way it is not good for humans to be alone, God needs community too, and He models perfect unity to us.

Ponder

Do you lean towards praying to one particular member of the Trinity? Do you think we should connect more with one of the three, with all of them equally, or with the unified whole?

Pray

Pray for unity in your family and unity among Christians, especially during this Christmas time.

DAY 31

When is Christmas?

Opening prayer

Mighty God, we praise You for dwelling among us and for providing for our daily needs. Amen.

Bible reading

Exodus 25:1–9; Hebrews 8:1–7

In most of the world, the commemoration of the birth of Jesus happens on 25 December, and has been celebrated on that day since around 300 years after the event. It is very unlikely that He was actually born on that day, but as ancient Pagan and Roman festivals were celebrated around the winter solstice, it made sense to join up the holidays. Similarly, Hannukah was celebrated around then. When we explore the more probable date of Jesus' birth, it would be likely that Mary *conceived* in December, so perhaps that is why we celebrate during this time.

I'd like to say first that the exact date doesn't really matter. It is more important that we mark and celebrate His coming than that we do so on the exact day it happened. However, getting the dating right might actually help broaden our understanding of what He came to do.

There are three festivals in the Old Testament that are the most important. These are when the people would gather in Jerusalem to mark them. Firstly, Passover (*Pesach*) commemorates the freedom of the people as they escaped slavery in Egypt, with lambs' blood on the doors as the angel of death passed over their homes. Secondly, Pentecost (*Shavuot*) happened as the first fruits of the harvest were gathered and given to God in thanksgiving, and marked the giving of God's law to the people (via Moses and stone tablets). Thirdly, the Feast of Tabernacles (*Sukkot*) was the main harvest festival and focused on remembering God's presence with the people as they lived in the desert and His provision of the manna they ate. They lived in tents and made the tabernacle (the tent sanctuary for God's presence) where He promised to live, in the midst of them.

The major events in Jesus' life match up with these three major Old Testament festivals as He fulfills each one. At Passover He achieves our freedom from the slavery of sin by his own bloodshed. At Pentecost the law of God is translated from stone tablets to writing on our hearts with the giving of the Holy Spirit. At the Feast of Tabernacles... well, God comes to dwell in the midst of his people – not in a tent, but in a human body. It is likely that Jesus was actually born at harvest time – so, September/October – when people were celebrating God's provision of the bread that kept them alive, and His presence among them. This may just be a point of interest, perhaps providing helpful context, but shouldn't shift the practice of thousands of years and the habits of millions of people! Happy Christmas!

Ponder

How much of our celebration of Christmas is cultural rather than biblical? Does it matter?

Pray

Pray that your friends and family would know the presence and provision of God this Christmas and in the coming year.

Group Study Notes

There are many ways to conduct a Bible study with others. Perhaps the most obvious is gathering together in person to talk and pray. This guide imagines you'll be able to do just that, every week, throughout the course of Advent.

If it's tough to find a time to get together, why not consider a group email discussion or another from of group chat (perhaps on WhatsApp, Skype or something similar)? Each person (or a leader) can post questions and thoughts that everyone can see and respond to. You might be able to work together daily on this basis, or as and when you can.

If you choose to gather in the traditional way, you might want to pick one or two of the characters from the days in that session to read aloud. Perhaps you could focus on the ones you found most interesting or challenging, or the ones that suit the topics you'd like to discuss. In a relaxed setting, you may want to discuss the session as a whole and see if a common favourite character emerges and then look at that one in more detail. Similarly, if any of the items to ponder or subjects for prayer were particularly poignant for someone in the group, it can be powerful to share those experiences and thoughts with others.

I'd like you to feel free to go wherever your response to the pieces takes you. An open discussion can lead to some profound places without any need for guidance. Sometimes a little steering may help. You may feel led to check something out that I've said and do some further research. Of course, if you want to just work through the following suggestions, then that's fine too.

Finally, pray. Pray in advance that the discussion will be helpful. Pray as you start for each person to be gracious and open. Pray that above all, God's would be the loudest voice in the room and in each heart.

SESSION ONE: EXPECTATION

Advent is a time of expectation. The Scriptures are also full of expectation for the coming of Jesus – both for the first time and His intended return. Expectation is a hopeful way of framing the less glamourous-sounding concept of 'waiting'. The Bible continually tells us to 'wait' for the Lord. These eight studies consider what we are expecting as we wait for Jesus – light in the darkness, His teaching and justice, answers to prayer, things beyond our imagination, being saved and being free. In this session, we found encouragement that He is already in the past, present and future, and have been insprired by Mary to be willing to serve Him in the waiting time.

Read
Psalm 37:1–40

Discuss
1. Do you think of yourself as a patient person, or do you struggle with waiting?
2. What are you waiting for, and what do you think the world is waiting for?
3. How can a relationship with God be helpful in times of waiting?
4. How can we turn waiting into expectation? How can we wait with hope?
5. Why do you think God gives us so many opportunities to wait and expect?
6. What do you think it will be like when Jesus comes again?

You could close by having each person share what their expectation is for this coming season, good or bad, and then praying for each other accordingly.

SESSION TWO: INCARNATION

The beauty of this time of year is in the remembrance of God becoming human. Jesus chooses to become like us and to live with us. He is gritty, earthly, fleshy and real. More to the point, He is here, not somewhere else. We have seen that His coming clarifies that God is our Father and shows us how the Bible fits together. His presence can give us confidence and joy, and it models values of humility, simplicity, care and sacrifice.

Read
Hebrews 2:11–18

Discuss
1. Is it helpful to think of Jesus as a brother?
2. Is it important to you that God understands what it is like to be human?
3. Does knowing Jesus change how you feel about death?
4. How does Jesus' mercy tie in with His humanity?
5. The devil is mentioned here, along with a reference to the temptation of Jesus. How does the incarnation trump Satan?
6. In what ways do you think it would have been different if Jesus had come to today's culture?

I think it is fun to imagine the humanity of Jesus. Do people in your group have an idea of what He was like to talk to? You could share thoughts about His sense of humour, or what may have been His favourite places and things to do. How does being God affect His humanity? Spend time praising Him however feels comfortable in your group – you could each share something about Him that you are thankful for, or read aloud a praise Psalm such as 148 or 150.

SESSION THREE: REPERCUSSION

It might be obvious to say it, but the coming of Jesus made an impact. It affected those around at the time, and it affects us still, in all sorts of ways. Over these few days, we've seen how Jesus' coming establishes His heavenly kingdom. He opens access to God for all people of all religions, He makes an eternal home accessible, He can understand and hold our grief, He loves the unlovable, conquers evil and brings peace. And that's just the beginning!

Read
Romans 8:31–39

Discuss
1. What does the coming of Jesus tell us about the nature of God?
2. Do you think about Jesus interceding for us? What do you think He asks of the Father?
3. What might be the repercussions of following Christ, good and bad?
4. What differences have you experienced in your life as a result of knowing Jesus?
5. Would you add or remove anything from the things that cannot separate us from God's love listed in Romans 8:38–39?
6. God's love is described as being 'in' Christ Jesus. How do you think that works?

What are the repercussions of Jesus' coming that matter most, at the moment, to the people in the room? Is there a situation or person they are praying for a lot? Join with them in praying that Jesus would have an impact there.

SESSION FOUR: REVERBERATION

The reverberations of the coming of Christ go on into eternity, not least as people continue to choose to follow Him. He makes a personal relationship with God possible, Jesus comes to save those who want to be saved, He brings wisdom and understanding, He opens the way for us to be baptised with the Spirit and He helps us understand the Trinity. And, of course, He has paved the way for His return...

Read
2 Peter 3:3–15

Discuss
1. How do you think God interacts with earthly time?
2. What do you think a 'holy and godly' life looks like?
3. How do we speed/hasten/hurry the day of the Lord?
4. Are you looking forward to the new heaven and the new earth?
5. 'The Lord's patience means salvation.' For whom?
6. Do you live in expectation of the promised second coming of Jesus?

This could be a good opportunity for one or two people to share testimonies of how they came to choose to follow Jesus and the difference it has made in their life. Why not close by considering what reverberations (the visible results) of Jesus' coming each person wants to see in their own life or community in the coming year? Spend some time praying that those reverberations would be realised.

Cover to Cover Bible Studies for Lent
Ideal for group or individual use

NEW TITLE

Living Faith: Invitations from the cross
by Krish Kandiah

Award-winning author Krish Kandiah brings his Bible knowledge and contemporary edge to this Lent Bible study guide. Explore the seven sayings of the cross and discover how these are a personal invitation from God, encouraging us to connect with Him on a deeper level.

ISBN: 978-1-78259-691-2

ALSO BY ABBY

At the Cross
by Abby Guinness

Approach the cross from a new direction during Lent by considering the perspectives of those present at Christ's crucifixion. Each of the six sessions includes Bible readings and fictional eyewitness monologues with textual and historical insights.

ISBN: 978-1-78259-498-7

Fleeting Shadows: How Christ transforms the darkness
by Malcolm Duncan

Malcolm Duncan draws from his own life experience to help us reflect on the cross and the power of Christ as we walk through challenging trials and tribulations.

ISBN: 978-1-78259-420-8

To find out about all our Lent titles, for current prices and to order, visit **www.cwr.org.org.uk/store**
Available online or from Christian bookshops.

SmallGroup central

*All of our small group ideas
and resources in one place*

Online:

www.smallgroupcentral.org.uk
is filled with free video teaching,
tools, articles and a whole host
of ideas.

On the road:

A range of seminars themed for
small groups can be brought to
your local community. Contact us at
hello@smallgroupcentral.org.uk

In print:

Books, study guides and DVDs
covering an extensive list of themes,
Bible books and life issues.

Find out more at:
www.smallgroupcentral.org.uk

Courses and events

Waverley Abbey College

Publishing and media

Conference facilities

Transforming lives

CWR's vision is to enable people to experience personal transformation through applying God's Wor to their lives and relationships.

Our Bible-based training and resources help people around the world to:
- Grow in their walk with God
- Understand and apply Scripture to their lives
- Resource themselves and their church
- Develop pastoral care and counselling skills
- Train for leadership
- Strengthen relationships, marriage and family life and much more.

Our insightful writers provide daily Bible reading notes and other resources for all ages, and our experienced course designers and presenters have gained an international reputation for excellence and effectiveness.

CWR's Training and Conference Centres in Surrey and East Sussex, England, provide excellent facilities in idyllic settings – ideal for both learning and spiritu refreshment.

CWR Applying God's Word
to everyday life and relationships

CWR, Waverley Abbey House,
Waverley Lane, Farnham,
Surrey GU9 8EP, UK

Telephone: **+44 (0)1252 784700**
Email: **info@cwr.org.uk**
Website: **www.cwr.org.uk**

Registered Charity No. 294387
Company Registration No. 1990308